The Laws of Christ:

Living the Way God Wants

Stan E. DeKoven

The Laws of Christ:

Living the Way God Wants

ISBN 978-1-61529-002-4

All scripture quotations taken from the New American Standard Version of the Bible unless otherwise noted.

Published by:

Vision Publishing
1115 D Street
Ramona, CA 92065
1-800-9-VISION
www.visionpublishingservices.com

Acknowledgments

I want to give special thanks to our students around the world who are studying diligently, and achieving greatness in the Kingdom of God. Further, I give thanks to those like me who have often struggled to understand what the Lord really requires of us, and how to live it. Also, to Reverends Gary and Gina Holley, my dear friends and partners in the training of men and women in the nations, true servants, who give me the privilege of giving input to their congregation on a regular basis. Finally, to my family, and co-workers at Vision, you are wonderful and I am blessed to have your support and love.

Forward By
Reverends Gary and Gina Holley

Dr. Stan DeKoven deals with four essential areas that Christ our Lord esteemed valuable in Matthew (chapter five). Every individual living for Christ faces the complexity of how they will deal with anger, purity, honesty and love. He walks you through an encounter with biblical and personal illustrations that enables a believer to clearly evaluate God's loving demand on their life.

We see that there is a misconception in the body of Christ regarding the issue of law in the church. Believers strongly adhere to their position that they are no longer under the law, but under grace alone. They are fifty percent correct and fifty percent wrong. We are definitely under grace, yet Christ never stated that we are no longer under the law. In fact, He emphasizes the command of God to fulfill the law.

Dr. DeKoven addresses this platform wonderfully, reinstating the joy of following the law because Gods Grace is active in us. Our church was blessed beyond measure to receive this kind of practical and essential teaching.

This book will cause you to shout "AMEN", laugh at our humanity, and weep at the need for change in our lives.

As you soak in the pages ahead with an open heart you will hear a fresh perspective that could possibly alter your mindsets and challenge you to redesign your life.

Pastors Gary and Gina Holley
Senior Pastors of F.C.F.I.M.

Table of Contents

The Laws of Christ

Introduction

In 2004, prompted by some personal study and I believe the Holy Spirit, I developed a series of messages titled "The Laws of Christ". I preached/ taught this as a four-part series for one church, Fontana Christian Center International, in Fontana, California. I have the privilege of serving this church as an advisor and friend, and as a co-laborer with Pastors Gary and Gina Holley and church family.

Upon completion of the series I felt (perhaps in the midst of over-exuberance), to take my notes from these messages and expand them into a small book, primarily for the FCCI congregation, as a gift to them for being such gracious hearers. If the book goes much further than that so be it; I have fulfilled my pledge in the writing and printing of this work.

I do hope, as do all Christian writers, that the book will enrich someone's life, and for the faithful congregants of FCCI will be a reminder of what has been taught and that a deepening of these vital concepts will ensue.

It is such a privilege to focus my teaching on foundational principles in a series called "The Laws of Christ". Our context for this teaching is found in Matthew 5; commonly called the *Beatitudes* or the

Sermon on the Mountain, and subsequent teachings. These teachings by Christ, no doubt repeated and embellished by him in His earthly ministry, were to fulfill and complete the Laws of Moses, for one greater than Moses was truly here, Jesus Christ. In this brief study we will look at four of the key laws of Christ; *Anger, Purity, Honesty, & Love.*

"And one of them, a lawyer, asked him a question, testing Him. Teacher, which is the great commandment in the Law? And He said to him,

You shall love the Lord your God with all your heart and with all your soul, and with all your mind.

This is the great and foremost commandment. And a second is like it,

You shall love your neighbor as yourself.

Matt. 22: 35-40

Laws of Christ

"And seeing the multitudes, he went up into the mountain: and when he had sat down, his disciples came to him: and he opened his mouth and taught them, saying, Blessed are the poor in spirit: for theirs is the kingdom of heaven. Blessed are they that mourn: for they shall be comforted. Blessed are the meek: for they shall inherit the earth. Blessed are they that hunger and thirst after righteousness: for they shall be filled. Blessed are the merciful: for they shall obtain mercy. Blessed are the pure in heart: for they shall see God. Blessed are the peacemakers: for they shall be called sons of God. Blessed are they that have been persecuted for righteousness' sake: for theirs is the kingdom of heaven. Blessed are ye when *men* shall reproach you, and persecute you, and say all manner of evil against you falsely, for my sake. Rejoice, and be exceeding glad: for great is your reward in heaven: for so persecuted they the prophets that were before you. You are the salt of the earth: but if the salt has lost its savor, wherewith shall it be salted? It is thenceforth good for nothing, but to be cast out and trodden under foot of men. You are the light of the world. A city set on a hill cannot be hid. Neither do *men* light a lamp, and put it under the bushel, but on the stand; and it shines unto all that are in the house. Even so let your light shine before men; that they may see your good works, and glorify your Father who is in heaven. Think not that I came to destroy the law or the prophets: I came not to destroy, but to fulfill. For verily I say unto you, Till heaven and earth pass, one jot or one tittle shall in no wise pass away from the law, till all things be accomplished. Whosoever therefore shall break one of these least commandments, and shall teach men so, shall be called least in the kingdom of heaven: but whosoever shall do and teach them, he shall be called great in the kingdom of heaven. For I say unto you, that except your righteousness shall exceed *the righteousness* of the scribes and Pharisees, ye shall in no wise enter into the kingdom of heaven. You have heard that it was said to them of old time, You shall not kill; and whosoever shall kill shall be in danger of the judgment: but I say unto you, That whosoever who is angry with his brother without a cause shall be in danger of the judgment: and whosoever shall say to his brother, Raca, shall be in danger of the council: but whosoever shall say, Thou fool, shall be in danger of hell fire. (Matt. 5: 1-22; KJV)

Introduction to the Laws of Christ

Jesus is addressing a crowd, but more specifically, he is teaching his precious and committed disciples. These eight characteristics of grace, which should be evident in every believer's life, speak of an upward climb in the spirit for the committed Christian. To fulfill the laws of Christ should be our highest desire, our truest aim.

Though there are innumerable possible lessons that could be taken from this power teaching of Christ, there are but four primary "laws of Christ" that I will focus on. Before looking at "The Law of Anger", it is important to provide the proper context from the scripture just presented.

Blessings for Kingdom Dwellers

There are special, unique and divinely powerful blessings (favor, happiness, grace) that are provided to us by our relationship with God through Christ. They are listed here for our contemplation and edification. These blessings are not restricted to the super-spiritual, but for all believers in Jesus Christ. Let's examine each with commentary.

- Highly favored are those who are **Poor in Spirit**. The poor in spirit are those who have become emptied of self. They have recognized that life is not all about us, all about our success, needs being met, etc. For in reality we are all ultimately helpless, for we are outside of God's presence (until we know Christ), and must have a broken and contrite heart (Ps. 51:17). We are highly favored by the Lord when we are able to acknowledge that but for the grace of God there go I, and that, without Christ in our lives, meaning and purpose will ultimately evade us. Remember, heaven is ours from the moment our poverty spirit, that is, our spirit devoid of the life of God in Christ, is made new, for in him we have life! See 2 Cor. 5:17

• Highly favored and full of God's grace are those who mourn, especially over our sin, knowing that in our mourning we will experience the comfort of the Holy Spirit. For those who have experienced great loss (as I have in the death of my first wife Karen), grief and mourning are essential for our restored health. For those who mourn, for sin, for loss, for the hard times, comfort is guaranteed to us. How sad for those who are unable or unwilling to mourn for missing the mark of God's high call in Christ Jesus, of becoming by His grace all He intended for us to be.

• There is often confusion when it comes to the concept of meekness. Jesus states here that the meek will inherit the earth (the realm of

God's rule, dominion with God). But one might ask, how can those who are down and out, wounded and discouraged, inherit? Well, *there* is the problem; not the word meek, but our understanding of the word and its work. Meekness means a gentle, quiet strength. If you will, the meek are those who rest in confidence that whatever might seem to be, whatever troubles might come, it is well with my soul. It is often true that the one with something to prove boasts the most. Those who know their God will do exploits (Dan 11: 32). Not the boastful, but those who are confident, faithful, fixed in their mind and heart on the goodness and provision of God will inherit the prosperity God intends for all His children. The meek will inherit, not heaven (that is for the poor in spirit), but the earth, and all that God has made available to us for a life of fulfillment and purpose.

• What a natural thing hunger and thirst are. We all experience these natural phenomena on a daily basis. But the hunger and *thirst* that the Lord is presenting here are more than a natural hunger for a good cob salad or the thirst for a diet coke (ok, some of my personal hunger and thirst becomes evident). He desires us to hunger and thirst for right. This hunger is manifested in our lives when we want what God wants, which is for us to desire to know God and to serve Him in all we do. Further, God wants us to agree with His standards for living, both in word and deed. Frankly, the church today is filled with people who, in agreement with James, are hearers of the word but not doers, who deceive themselves. To hunger for God is to want to be in His presence, but more importantly, it is to do His will. In doing so, we receive fulfillment in this life, even as we prepare ourselves for eternity.

- Oh, to have a heart that does not condemn us. There are so many things people hold onto from the past; mistakes made, willful sin committed. In Christ, because of the shed blood of our precious Savior, we do not stand condemned before Him. We are forgiven. One of the keys to a solid and fruitful life in Christ is enjoying the reality that our sins, past, present and future are already forgiven, having been nailed to the cross of Christ, and therefore we have and can walk in the blessing of a **Pure Heart**. This reality (that we are cleansed of guilt and shame free) is so important that a separate chapter will be devoted to this subject later in this book.

- There is a phrase from an old hymn that comes to mind as I think about the next blessing of our life in Christ; "peace, peace, wonderful peace, coming down from the Father above". Peacemakers; wonderful folks they are. Peacemakers; of which Jesus is the chief of all, are those who are already pure in their hearts towards God, living a peaceful life towards men (peaceable disposition; not argumentative), having become like God, who is our peace, and has made peace between us and himself through Christ. There is a special blessing for those who, with grace flowing out of a heart filled with the spirit of peace, can bring others into the experience of peace with God and others.

- Well, up until now the blessings are fairly easy to bear. No real problem in that which has preceded us. However, one must ask the question: how can there be blessing in persecution, or in being reviled (mistreated)? Well, Jesus specifically states that those persecuted for right living will experience a full measure of the Kingdom of Heaven (which I accept as synonkymous with the Kingdom of God)) or the full measure of maturity. Whether we like it or not, we grow most during times of trial and testing. Even when people mistreat us, we can experience the privilege of suffering for Christ, which will release joy. Most of the church today is looking desperately for happiness. Happiness is transitory, but joy, the abiding presence and assurance of the Lord's pleasure in our lives, is abiding and sustaining.

In Summary

Remember, Jesus did not come to destroy the moral law, but to fulfill it. Greater than Moses, he took the law from outside requirements to an inner dynamic that would produce an outward change. These laws of Christ are not grievous ones. We can readily keep these laws by the grace or favor of God, and by the full measure of the Spirit of Christ that lives within us.

"Be angry, and yet do not sin; do not let the sun go down on your anger, and do not give the devil an opportunity."
Eph. 4: 26-27

" Whate'er begun in anger, ends in shame."
Benjamin Franklin,
Poor Richards Almanac, 1734

The Laws of Christ

Part I
The Law of Anger

Again, let us review the scripture that deals with the important issue of anger.

> "You have heard that the ancients were told, You 'SHALL NOT COMMIT MURDER' and 'whoever commits murder shall be liable to the court.' (Matt. 5:21-22)

What is anger? Anger is defined as a strong feeling of displeasure, wrath, rage, ire, fury. A psychological definition of anger states that it is a biological response to frustration, hurt or fear. The problem with anger is not anger (Eph. 4:26), but the person's heart attitude who is experiencing the anger, and how that anger is expressed toward others.

Within the context of the teachings of Christ, some interpreters, finding Jesus' teaching too difficult, add "without cause", but that is a disputed interpretation, as it is in some manuscripts but not all. We are not to get angry, even at those with empty heads (Raca), or the radically foolish (Fools).

Both of the words used by Jesus were common terms of derision; a desire to rid ourselves of our irritant was condemned as equal to murder. As many studies demonstrate and common sense dictates, anger is often the root of murder. Thus, we must:

- Be concerned with more than outward acts but intentions as well. We often judge others by their action, but ourselves and our friends by our/their intentions.

- Remember, what we *are*, is more important than what we *do* ("out of the abundance of heart, the mouth speaks" Matt.12:34). Sadly it is frequently seen that people are more interested in charisma than character. God is more interested in character than charisma, though both are needed to fulfill God's intention.

- Face the fact that to have no evil thought towards others is impossible ... outside of the righteousness of God "in Christ". Since we will all at times struggle with seeing others as air-headed ningnongs (an Aussie-ism), we must be willing to deal with our anger to avoid the consequences of anger denied or anger projected. That is, processing ones anger, without either pretending that one is not angry when one is, or exploding on others is healthy and beneficial.

- Finally, realize that Christ's claim on us is

for His reign to be over us in all things: God is to reign in our hearts, not just over our behavior: <u>We are in Christ...Christ is in us.</u>

How should we respond to the reality of anger?

First, Jesus states we are to:

- Go to our brother, with a focus on the restoration of the relationship. Of course, we should take caution. Not every wrong thought needs to be verbalized to an unsuspecting brother or sister in Christ. Most wrong attitudes or hurtful thoughts must be "cast down or taken captive". (2 Cor. 10:3-6) We must avoid the guilt-transferring activity of "dumping" our anger on someone who does not know we are even angry with them or offended by them. This can be the height of cruelty. Deal with that yourself, and only if something is "in the open" do you need to restore a relationship with your confession.

- Remember that humility overcomes rage. By humility, I mean to have an honest appraisal of yourself in light of God, His word, and others. In truth, none of us are perfect, all people make mistakes, and we must learn the grace of quick forgiveness if we are to enjoy the blessings of peace. Thus, let Christ be the judge, not self. We are not very good at it!

Conclusion

The Pharisees minded only the outside, Christ cares about the inside (godliness). They sought the praise and applause of men; we are to seek the approval of God. They were proud of their religion; we trust in His righteousness. We are unprofitable servants, relying on the grace and mercy of God.

*"A good name is to be more desired than great
riches, favor is better than silver and gold."*
Prov. 22:1

*"Integrity without knowledge is weak and useless,
and knowledge without integrity is dangerous and
dreadful."*
Samuel Johnson

The Laws of Christ

Part II
The Law of Honesty

"Again, you have heard that the ancients were told, 'YOU SHALL NOT MAKE FALSE VOWS, BUT SHALL FULFILL YOUR VOWS TO THE LORD.' "But I say to you, make no oath at all, either by heaven, for it is the throne of God, or by the earth, for it is the footstool of His feet, or by Jerusalem, for it is THE CITY OF THE GREAT KING. "Nor shall you make an oath by your head, for you cannot make one hair white or black. "But let your statement be, 'Yes, yes' or 'No, no; anything beyond these is of evil. (Matt. 5: 33-37)

Introduction

In a 1980's song, Billy Joel sings passionately, "Honesty seems to be the only word." But in the movie encounter between Tom Cruz and Jack Nicholson (A Few Good Men, 1992), to the question, "Do you want the truth?" the retort came, "You can't handle the truth." Honesty or truth is a difficult topic to discuss in our highly pluralistic, relativistic culture, where any absolute is suspect. But in Jesus' day as in ours, honesty and truth are essential qualities to obtain and emulate.

Again, we see Jesus addressing His disciples on this important topic. Before looking at "The Law of Honesty", let's give the context. Honesty is defined as being truthful, trustworthy, sincere, genuine, gained by fair means, frank and open (Dictionary.com).

Jesus used two Greek words to express the need for honesty. One is *kalos*, which means beautiful, good, valuable, virtuous, honest, worthy. The other is *semnos*, which means venerable (worthy of respect or reverence because of age, dignity), grave, honest. Then Jesus illustrated his teaching by referring to the way people often used an oath to practice deception. He told them – " Say no to oath taking. This was a common activity; to take oaths binding only to the degree that an object sworn by was thought to be holy. Thus, they could violate one oath (like the important duty of taking care of one's parents) with another oath, thus violating God's Word, being guilty of violating the law, and though guilty, their attempt was to avoid guilt. Thus, they would avoid caring for parents, which the law required, by saying that a certain amount of money was dedicated to the temple (when they died) thus they were not responsible to honor the parents by taking care of them financially...a simple but grievous manipulation for personal gain. The problem of that generation, of attempting to manipulate the word of God for ones benefit continues to this day.

The truth is, if one has to give an oath before his or

her word can be trusted, what a sad commentary. This type of manipulation should immediately convict our hearts as sinners, and motivate us towards right action.

How often have you heard someone tell you "I have to honest here?" It should provoke the question, "what have you been telling me up until now?" The truth is, a righteous man does not need oaths, for his word is his bond. How sad that in our modern world, even in Christian business and marriage, we must have contracts, even pre-nuptial agreements before entering into sacred and solemn relationships.

What then should we do to counteract this trend in our modern culture, and become people of honesty as God and civilization require? Here are 7 keys to honest living.

The Bible discusses many important attitudes and actions for the believer. They include:

- Having balanced scales, necessary to avoid taking advantage of, or cheating someone. (Le. 19:35-36) It is sad to see how often men and women of God will do things to their advantage and to the disadvantage of another, without even a sense of guilt or shame. This is a result of a seared or inadequate conscience, and should be purged by repentance.

- According to Romans 12:17, we should never pay pack evil for evil. Frankly, the process of taking revenge takes great energy, energy needed to live life as God has intended. Further, revenge is truly dishonest, as it is predicated on the premise that somehow we deserve and the other does not. Of course, it is true that we never forgive innocent people. None are; including us.

- Honesty in relationships is possible when we recognize that we are under the Banner of Love of Christ, and if we live without owing anything to others except to love them. (Rom. 13:8) When we recognize that God is watching over us (or if you have to, think of how you would feel if your mother or father found out what you were doing!) you will tend toward the honest, and when you sense an obligation to love without strings, honesty becomes an outgrowth.

- In 2 Peter 3:14, blameless diligence is a key to living a life of honesty. To be diligent one must stay focused on truth, pursue it with a whole heart, and when finding oneself straying in any way, ruthlessly return to the straight path. We are blameless when we do all we can with all we know, which is what we are ultimately held accountable for.

- Along with diligence, we need to be faithful stewards of all God has given us. In fact, if we are not a good steward of what others entrust to us, we will rarely be a good and faithful steward of what we have. It is a beautiful thing to see a faithful steward, one who works to his or her own hurt to make sure all is done well. (1 Corinthians. 4:2)

- There are great benefits in the long run when we live a life of integrity. (2 Kings 12:15) Integrity means honesty, and an honest person will be one who has integrity, or the ability to do things in an integrated or well rounded and complete manner.

- Finally, if for no other reason, being honest should be attempted by all of us as it will likely provide the means to a better income. (Proverbs 16:8) A better income or prosperity may not come instantaneously, as few of us will obtain riches or wealth at all, let alone swiftly, but we know that the Lord will provide for us, and peace and prosperity tend to follow those who are faithful in life and service to God. Prosperity follows the formula of hard work plus a bit of luck and God's favor over time.

"Who may ascend into the hill of the Lord? And who may stand in His holy place? He who has clean hands and a pure heart, who has not lifted up his soul to falsehood, and has not sworn deceitfully."
Psalms 24:3-4

"Simplicity reaches out to God; purity discovers and enjoys him."
Thomas a' Kempis

The Laws of Christ

Part III
The Law of Purity

"You have heard that it was said, 'YOU SHALL NOT COMMIT ADULTERY'; but I say to you that everyone who looks at a woman with lust for her has already committed adultery with her in his heart. 'If your right eye makes you stumble, tear it out and throw it from you; for it is better for you to lose one of the parts of your body, than for your whole body to go into hell. 'It was said, 'WHOEVER SENDS HIS WIFE AWAY, LET HIM GIVE HER A CERTIFICATE OF DIVORCE'; but I say to you that everyone that divorces his wife, except for the reason of unchastity, makes her commit adultery; and whoever marries a divorced woman commits adultery. (Matthew 5: 27-32)

Introduction

I really cannot remember how many times I prayed that God would purify my heart. There were so many issues, too many to discuss without the anonymity of a counselor or priest. I know this scripture so well. What condemnation, since I knew my heart (especially as an adolescent), and I knew how difficult it was for me to keep my heart and mind on the things above. (Col. 1) But try I might, and struggle I did. Often I asked myself, could anyone fulfill the requirement of a mind that never thought wrongly about another. In reality, according to Jesus, everyone I knew had violated His "new law", which I hardly saw as a law of love. But I was young, and did not understand the teaching in context, as many today still fail to do. That is why, to avoid condemnation and needless concerns, we must see this passage in its proper context. Again, before looking at "The Law of Purity", a look at the scripture in context will help in our understanding.

First of all, purity can be defined as: being free from adulterating or extraneous matter; pure, free from contamination, pollution or dirt, clean, innocent (Dictonary.com). The Greek word is *Katharos,* which also means clean, clear, pure.

As with the rest of the Beatitudes, Jesus was specifically dealing with issues of the heart that may (and generally do) manifest in overt behavior.

He develops the important concept that lust, which is uncontrolled passions or greed begins in heart/mind, not in the acted out behavior. All behavior begins in the mind or in thought, so we can rightly say that a seed sown will reap an eventual harvest, whether the seed is positive (God's word, love, etc.) of negative (criticism and condemnation, etc.). Fruit will be produced after its kind, over time. Sadly, many men and women believe (falsely) that they can sow negative seed into their hearts and minds and avoid the consequences. This is truly not so, and those who believe it are caught in the most heinous sin of all, pride, which leads to the inevitable fall. Let me illustrate this with a true story.

At one time Benjamin[1] had been an Elder in a local church. He was a staunch and faithful member, with a sterling reputation. He did carry a secret that eventually lead to deep waters. His wife of 15 years had developed a progressively worse case of alcohol abuse, which caused degeneration in the relationship. He took her privately to re-habilitation, tried all he knew to protect her and help, but one day she left him, running off with another man, never to return.

Naturally, Benjamin was distraught. He spiraled into a depression, stepped off the Elder board, and over a period of a year or two left attending church altogether, and moved to another town. About a year later, having changed jobs and beginning to recover, he began to attend church (no longer being mad at God for the situation that the Lord had not caused). Soon thereafter he met a younger woman to whom he was attracted, and the attraction was returned. Carol was new to the area, but was not a believer, seemingly a seeker. Within a short time, he set his eyes on her as the answer to his

---

[1] The names and situations have been altered for the sake of anonymity, but the story is true.

loneliness and hurt; she moved in with him leading to deeper destruction. When Benjamin finally hit bottom, he was virtually penniless, having spent all his money to try and make Carol happy, and in the end she left him for another.

To Benjamin's benefit, he finally faced the truth about his pride and lust, which had begun in his mind, and fully repented. His life now has true hope, for the power of lust is great, but the power of a repented heart, submitted to Christ is greater.

For many, the teaching of Jesus in this passage is most problematic, for who can measure up to His standard? Jesus was not condemning in the specific sense, only in the universal sense, that is, He was placing everyone on the same playing field. All human beings have a choice to make, and all must deal with where and on what they will place their affections.

When Jesus suggests what to do if a part of your anatomy offends you or causes you to stumble, he was not commanding self-mutilation. To cut something off or out of our lives indicates the need for self-denial, having made a realistic appraisal of the right and wrong of our intentions. Thus, we will have a focused intention on acceptance of God's plan and purpose for our lives (a people of purity). In a similar vein, He discusses the prickly issue of divorce and remarriage. Essentially, Jesus was stating that divorce and adultery are linked to the same root (not seeing as God does). Divorce so as to marry another is rooted in lust, with a desire to legitimize it through marriage. Both of these issues of the heart are common and will likely be faced at one time or another in our lives. Does Christ condemn us? No, but certainly our own choices can justify or condemn. Well, this requires the question, what shall we do? Let me suggest three responses that can help us to overcome and live a life of purity before God – follow the Way; the Truth; and the Life.

First of all, we should **desire the way** or path of Jesus. Living a life devoted to God is not all that hard, and is certainly reasonable. Jesus chose a life of submission to the Father and His Word. For we mere mortals, this may be a daily choice, but it can be done, and we can encourage each other in the process.

Secondly, we can **choose to live the truth**, that is, to desire God's generally accepted truth in our lives, essentially denying denial. To face the truth we must learn honesty in self appraisal. God's word states that we should buy truth and never sell it (Proverbs 23:23), recognizing that intimacy with The Truth (Jesus) and truth in general will be what liberates us from the impure. When we look at ourselves in the mirror of God's word, we must be willing to allow the Holy Spirit to reveal His intention for us. Once his intention is discerned, and if we do not line up with his word, we must be willing to repent, or change our thinking, which will lead to a change of lifestyle.

Thirdly, when we **walk the path** He gives us and live in light of the truth of God's word, we experience the **Life** he desires for us. Thus, we must choose to know and follow the word of God to the best of our ability, which is essential truly to enjoy life and its fullness. Real life means living in the liberty of Christ. It is a life celebrated, since we know we are forgiven, are eternally alive with our wonderful Lord, and have the opportunity to experience His abundance here as we walk in His will day by day. A life of purity is a life filled with joy, having a conscience cleared by His wonderful grace.

"Love is love's reward."
Dryden

"God is love."
John the Apostle

"If you love me, keep my commandments."
Jesus Christ

The Laws of Christ

Part IV
The Law of Love

"You have heard that it was said, 'AN EYE FOR AN EYE, AND A TOOTH FOR A TOOTH.' "But I say to you, do not resist an evil person; but whoever slaps you on your right cheek, turn the other to him also. "If anyone wants to sue you and take your shirt, let him have your coat also. "Whoever forces you to go one mile, go with him two. "Give to him who asks of you, and do not turn away from him who wants to borrow from you. "You have heard that it was said, 'YOU SHALL LOVE YOUR NEIGHBOR AND HATE YOUR ENEMY.' "But I say to you, love your enemies and pray for those who persecute you, so that you may be sons of your Father who is in heaven; for He causes His sun to rise on the evil and the good, and sends rain on the righteous and the unrighteous. "For if you love those who love you, what reward do you have? Do not even the tax collectors do the same? "If you greet only your brothers, what more are you doing than others? Do not even the Gentiles do the same? "Therefore you are to perfect, as your heavenly Father is perfect. (Matthew 5: 38-48)

Introduction

To love God makes perfect sense; He created us, cares for us, provides for us…what's not to love? To love our friends whom we enjoy spending time with, seems most reasonable, since we always care for those who care for us. But to love the unlovely, the enemy of my family and me, those who neither agree with my theology or politics? Now you are pushing it. And yes, Jesus was clearly pushing the issue of love on His disciples beyond what seemed remotely reasonable or necessary for them, let alone us.

The Law of Love as stated by Christ is by far the most difficult of all. Controlling my anger is a task but manageable. Being honest is really, well, between me and God, and doable with some effort. Purity is truly a high standard, but since I genuinely love my wife and have reached 50 years, I struggle rarely with the impure. But love your enemies. Well, grace, grace, grace is the need, if even grace can help me achieve this level of spiritual maturity. Again, before looking at **"The Law of Love"**, giving some context will help us to decipher this truly prickly issue. First let's define love.

In our only too inadequate Western dictionary, love is defined as strong affection, or a liking for someone or something; finally, a passionate affection for the opposite sex.

As most readers know, the Greek language of the day was nearly as expressive as our modern English. The word used here by Jesus is the Greek word *agape*, signifying God-like love or true benevolence, which is defined as the tendency to be kind, a generous act. In Greek, four words for love are used in different places, all of which are important and legitimate. They are:

- *Eros*, meaning erotic or sensual love.

- *Philia*, connoting brotherly/sisterly love, a deep bond of affection between people of the same or opposite gender.

- *Storge*, meaning family or covenantal love, like one would have for mother or father, and such as is common amongst workmates and congregants.

- *Agape*, which is characterized by unselfish, other-oriented love, looking out for the best interest of the other; good will. This is the focus of the word Jesus uses here.

As in previous cases, Jesus is teaching by way of illustration. The primary issue Jesus was dealing with was *authority* and *submission* (to legitimate authority). He was not advocating the type of submission to authority demanded by strict fundamentalist cults and by some non-Christian religions such as radical Islam, where absolute blind obedience is slavishly required. Obedience and submission are a necessary component of love. But we must show caution. For Jesus is clearly stating that our submission is to legitimate authority. For example, in John 18:19, 24, Jesus is confronted by the High Priest, yet Jesus stands up for his right to speak. Further, Paul used his citizen rights to avoid a flogging and perhaps worse. (see Acts 25:11-12). In this passage, Jesus *is* using a fairly radical metaphor to illustrate an important truth. He is stating that our love must extend beyond what seems reasonable if we are to emulate the love of God. However, our love is to be for Righteousness' sake. That is, for the sake of righteousness, we do not resist legitimate authority, or because it is for a right or just cause. Further, we give without demanding compensation or accolade (we go the extra mile), simply because it is right and pleases our Father. Finally, we do not seek revenge, but instead trust God to deal with those who may have hurt us in some way.

Jesus' concern was action, not feeling. That is, He does not expect us to have touchy feely sentiment towards someone who has taken advantage of us or used us in some way. It would be unnatural to feel happy about such things. He does, however, expect His children to do what is right in spite of how we might feel. That is the true test of love. When we do not seem to be getting our prayers answered, or the prosperity we desire, do we pray anyway, give anyway, and serve anyway? ...that is love for God. If our family does not seem to notice our efforts to bless, care for, assist them, in fact, when it seems as though all they do is use us for their benefit, do we still care and share with wisdom and grace? When a competitor in business, or a boss treats us wrongly, do we continue to serve to the best of our ability? Do we put our trust in the Lord that he will work all things according to the counsel of His will, and on our behalf? If we do, we are coming close to loving our neighbor. Finally, are you able to be gracious to sister Wippendiddle when she tells you how wrong you are for being whom God has made you to be? If so, you are exercising the love of God in church. This is, for many, one of the most difficult arenas in which to express true love.

In all relationships, we are to love, forgive, give, and care. For none of the ones we love, forgive, care for are really deserving ... but neither are we. It is truly because of who Jesus is and what He has done for us that we are to live and move and have our very being. We love God and others because he first loved us.

Thus, as difficult as it may seem, Jesus is commanding us to live in these four principles by:

- Dealing with anger, which we can do by His grace ...

- Living in purity, or walking daily in the knowledge of His presence ...

- Walking in honesty, having open and covenantal relationships pleasing to the Lord ... and

- Loving like God loves, by looking beyond feelings and attempting to achieve one's own vindication, and releasing others from judgment, so that we in turn can enjoy the freedom of a life without judgment.

Conclusion

It must have taken a few days or even weeks for the shock of the words of Christ to sink in to His disciples. The impact was no doubt life changing. Of course, the full implementation of the teaching was not tested until after Christ's death, burial, resurrection, and ascension. Perhaps this is a reason – knowing the improbability of keeping the laws He presented, Jesus urged the disciples to wait for power from on high. Without Holy Spirit power in our lives, living according to His principles would be exceedingly difficult. But with Christ in us, the hope of glory, we can truly do all things.

Other Books by the Author

Assessment in Counseling
Christian Education
Crisis Counseling
Family Violence
40 Days to the Promise
Fresh Manna
From A Father's Heart
Grief Relief
Healing Community
Homiletics
I Want to be Like You Dad
Journey Through the New Testament
Journey Through the Old Testament
Journey to Wholeness
Living Fruitfully
Marriage and Family Life
New Beginnings
On Belay!
Parenting on Purpose
Pastoral Ministry
Prelude to a Requiem
Research Writing Made Easy
Strategic Church Administration
Supernatural Architecture
That's the Kingdom of God
Transferring the Vision
Twelve Steps to Wholeness
Visionary Leadership